306·362
3264

£ 1549676

About this book

The story of the slave trade is one of the most terrible in our history. For over two hundred and fifty years, traders forced millions of men, women and children out of Africa and sold them into slavery in the New World. These slaves helped to build up the wealth of England and America. But they got none of it themselves.

The pictures in this book show you how the slave trade worked. You can see auction posters and bills of sale written by the traders. There are also pictures which were drawn by people who tried to stop the trade. They show what it was like to travel on a slave ship, to be sold at an auction and to work on a plantation in America. There have always been people, black and white, who saw that it was wrong for one man to own another. You can learn how they slowly changed the way most people thought.

Some of the words printed in *italics* may be new to you. You can look them up in the word list on page 92.

AN EYEWITNESS BOOK

The Slave Trade

ANNE MOUNTFIELD

WAYLAND PUBLISHERS LONDON

More Eyewitness Books

Country Life in the Middle Ages   Penelope Davies
Town Life in the Middle Ages   Penelope Davies
The Tudor Family   Ann Mitchell
The Printer and his Craft   Helen Wodzicka
The Age of Drake   Leonard W. Cowie
The Story of the Wheel   Peter Hames
Newgate to Tyburn   Jane Dorner
Growing Up in the Middle Ages   Penelope Davies
Children of the Industrial Revolution   Penelope Davies
A Victorian Sunday   Jill Hughes
Markets and Fairs   Jane Dorner
Livingstone in Africa   Denis Judd
Florence Nightingale   Philippa Stewart
The Mayflower Pilgrims   Brenda Colloms
The Voyages of Captain Cook   Roger Hart
Stagecoach and Highwayman   Stephanie McKnight
The Railway Builders   Alistair Barrie
Men in the Air   Roger Hart
The Glorious Age of Charles II   Helen Wodzicka

Frontispiece: A slave gang marching to the West African coast.

SBN 85340 205 1
Copyright © 1973 by Wayland Publishers Ltd
101 Grays Inn Road, London, WC1
Filmset by Keyspools Ltd, Golborne, Lancs
Printed and bound by C. Tinling & Co Ltd, Prescot, Lancs

Contents

Out of Africa

This book is about the Atlantic slave trade. For hundreds of years, European traders took black men out of Africa and shipped them across the Atlantic Ocean. The Africans were forced to work as slaves for white settlers in America and the West Indies. At least fifteen million Africans were sold into slavery this way. That is about twice the number of people living in London today.

Slavery itself was nothing new. There had been slaves in Greek and Roman times. Africans made their prisoners-of-war into slaves. They sold many of them to Arab traders long before the Europeans came. Even today, in some far corners of the world, slaves are bought and sold. But it was the Atlantic slave trade that took millions of black people to America to work as the slaves of a white race.

The Portuguese were among the first Europeans to trade in African slaves. Portuguese seamen began to sail to the west coast of Africa about 1420. They traded guns, iron, cloth and liquor with the African chiefs. In return, the chiefs offered gold, ivory, spices—and slaves. The Portuguese shipped the slaves back to Lisbon and sold them. Like most people of that time, the Portuguese thought there was nothing wrong in making *pagans* into slaves. They hoped they could make the pagans become Christians. They sent some of the first Negro slaves as a gift to the Pope.

CHRISTOPHER COLUMBUS. When Christopher Columbus sailed from Spain in 1492, he was searching for a new sea route to the East. Instead, he discovered the islands in the Caribbean Sea. He had already explored the west coast of Africa, and he had taken Africans to work on his ship. As you can see in the picture opposite, some of his sailors were Negroes. His pilot, Pedro Nino, was black. In 1498, Columbus took on a shipload of African slaves and brought them to Hispaniola to work for the first Spanish settlers.

AFRICAN SOCIETY. The map above belonged to another of Columbus's pilots. Compare it with a modern map of Africa. You will see that people really didn't know what this continent looked like. When Columbus sailed to Africa, many African empires were breaking up into tribes. But there were still great cities, like Benin, on the west coast. It stands in ruins today. The Africans had their own culture and customs. They were skilled in leather and iron work, carpentry and farming. They had their own religion, music and art.

9

INDIAN SLAVES. In the 16th century, many Spanish noblemen and fortune-hunters set sail for America. They hoped to find a land rich in gold and silver. The Spaniards made the American "Indians" into slaves and treated them cruelly. This picture shows the Spaniards savagely beating them. Thousands of Indians died from starvation and over-work.

THE FIRST PLANTATIONS. Some Europeans set-
tled on islands in the Caribbean Sea. They set up huge
plantations where they grew sugar cane, and forced
the Indians to become their slaves. This picture shows
slaves bringing the sugar cane to the mill. The mill
squeezed out the juice and then it was boiled down
into sugar crystals. The sticky *molasses* which were
left over were distilled to make rum. The slaves worked
eighteen hours a day, six days a week. Thousands
were worked to death. The settlers wanted more
slaves—slaves from Africa.

SIR JOHN HAWKINS. John Hawkins was a daring English seaman who lived during the time of Queen Elizabeth I (1558–1603). He knew that he could make a fortune by trading for slaves on the West African coast and selling them to Spanish planters in America. England and Spain were at war, but Hawkins risked sailing in Spanish waters to bring slaves to the Spanish settlers. He made three slaving voyages. On the third, his cousin Francis Drake went with him. The Spaniards attacked them as pirates and they narrowly escaped death.

ENGLISH COLONIES. England began to set up her own colonies in the New World. In the time of James I (1603—25) and Charles I (1625—49), Englishmen began to settle in the West Indies and North America. Many white settlers came to the New World as *indentured labourers.* They sold themselves into slavery for seven years. In return, their masters paid their fare. During the Civil War, Oliver Cromwell got rid of many prisoners by sending them to the West Indies. This picture shows the Battle of Worcester which took place in 1651. After Cromwell won the battle, he shipped 7,000 Scottish prisoners-of-war to Barbados to work as indentured labourers.

THE SUGAR ISLANDS. More and more English settlers arrived in the West Indies and in North America. Some of them were Royalists who had fought on the side of Charles I during the Civil War. This old map shows the islands of the West Indies. The settlers here grew tobacco, rice, indigo and cotton on their plantations. In 1645, colonists in the Barbados began to grow sugar. The planters made big profits, but they needed lots of men to work the sugar cane. Like the Spanish, they wanted slaves from Africa.

SLAVING COMPANIES. Charles II became King in 1660. He set up a company of merchants to trade with the Africans for slaves. The merchants called themselves the Company of Royal Adventurers, and Charles II minted a new coin in their honour. You can see the coin on this page. It was made from African gold and showed the King's head and an African elephant. It was called the Guinea, because that was the name of the West African coast where slaves were traded.

WHITE BUYERS. The first European slave traders just raided the African coast for slaves. They tempted the Africans right up to the gang-planks of their ships by showing them strange objects—pieces of red cloth or brightly-coloured beads. Later, the sailors traded for slaves with the African chiefs, as the picture above shows. The merchant companies made big profits on the deals. Cheap iron bars were used as money in Africa. The sailors exchanged them for slaves worth many pounds.

TRADING BEGINS. When the European slave ships reached the African coast, they anchored off-shore. The captain or his mate went ashore to trade with the chief, as you can see in the picture opposite. The Europeans showed great respect to the native chiefs. Sometimes, the Africans sent canoes out to trade with the sailors on board ship. The carpenter turned the largest cabin into a shop, and the sailors put all the trading goods on display. Then the carpenter fitted out the hold for the new cargo—the slaves.

AFRICAN TRADERS.   Some chiefs became greedy.
They liked the muskets and cheap rum which the
sailors traded for slaves. So they attacked neigh-
bouring villages, or even their own tribe, for slaves
to sell. Chiefs sent their slave hunters to set fire to
villages at night. The hunters captured the young and
strong villagers as they fled in terror from their
blazing huts. They marched the captured slaves in
a "coffle", or chain gang, to the Guinea coast.

BRANDING.   This sailor is branding a slave woman.
He is using a red-hot iron to burn onto her skin the
initials of the trading company which has bought her.
Before the sailors bought her, they examined her to
make sure she was under thirty-five years old, healthy,
with good eyes and teeth, and no grey hairs. If her
hair had been grey, the African traders might have
shaved her head before they sold her. She will be
branded again in America by her new owner.

FORTS. Most European countries set up forts along the African coast to protect their slave trade. This picture shows one of the first forts the Portuguese built on the Guinea coast of Africa. By the 18th century, slave trading was an organized business between black *agents* and white agents who lived on the African coast. The whites were a rough and drunken lot. Many died of fever—as this old verse about the Benin Coast shows:

"Beware and Take Care of the Bight of Benin.
There's one comes out for forty goes in."

SLAVE "FACTORIES". The valuable human cargo was stored in a place called a "factory" before it was shipped to America. This is a "barracoon", a wooden stockade where the men slaves were kept in chains. The women were left free to make the food. Many slaves never reached the factories—they died on the long march to the coast. More slaves died at the factories from fever or cruel treatment, before the slave ships arrived to take on this fresh stock of "Black Ivory."

The Middle Passage

Most of Europe began to trade in slaves. England, Portugal, France, Holland, Sweden, Denmark—all of them had fortresses on the coast of Africa and fought for the right to supply New World settlers with slaves.

By the end of the 18th century, English ships had gained the right to carry almost half of the slaves who crossed the Atlantic. Some slave ships sailed from London or Bristol, but by 1800 three-quarters of them sailed from Liverpool. In 1794, 138 Liverpool ships were in the trade with nearly 4,000 sailors aboard.

When you see how the slaves were packed into the stinking, suffocating holds of slave ships, you may wonder how people could be so cruel. The ship owners and traders who made great profits from this human cargo were often kindly family men. They spent some of their profits to build the railways and set up new industries like cotton-weaving and iron. They used the rest of the money to collect beautiful furniture and paintings for their homes.

Only very few people disapproved of the slave trade and tried to change it. Most people saw nothing wrong. They thought the slaves were different from themselves. They did not believe that slaves felt pain and sorrow as they did. The "good" slave captains tried to keep their shiploads healthy and cheerful. The bad ones were greedy and overloaded their ships to make bigger profits. But people thought that ill-treating slaves was no better and no worse than ill-treating a dog or a horse.

LOADING.   The wretched Africans were packed in
a canoe, like the one in the picture above, and taken
to a slave ship. Many of them had never seen the sea
or white men before. Some slaves thought white men
were devils who were going to eat them. The sailors
thought that was funny and tried to make all of them
believe it. A few slaves were so terrified that they
tried to kill themselves. They swallowed handfuls of
earth on the quayside or jumped overboard and
drowned.

THE SLAVE DECKS.   The ship in the picture on the
right is taking on a load of slaves. Sometimes, the
slaves were kept chained in the hold for seven or
eight months while the ship sailed from one part of
the coast to another picking up more human cargo.
In rough weather, the hatches to the slave decks were
shut tight and the slaves often suffocated. Sometimes
the ship's surgeon could not take care of the dying
because he could not get his candle to burn in the
airless hold.

THE "MIDDLE PASSAGE." The slave ships made a triangular voyage which you can see marked on this map. English traders loaded up their boats at home with cheap goods and took them to Africa. There they traded the goods for slaves. The dreaded "Middle Passage" was the voyage across the Atlantic with the slaves packed in the ships' holds. They were sold in America and the West Indies. To complete the triangle, the ships took West Indian sugar and rum, and American cotton and tobacco back to England.

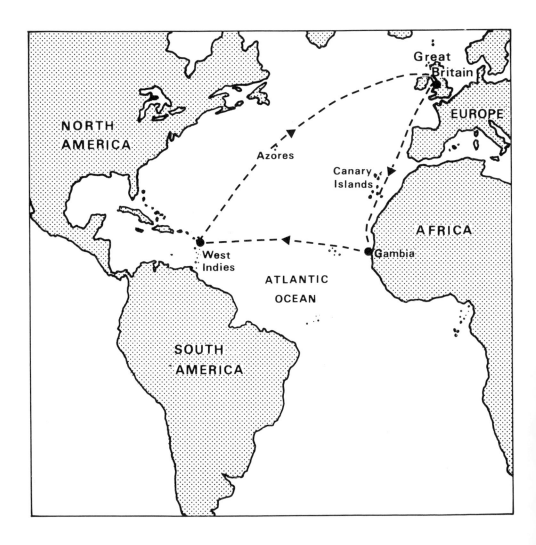

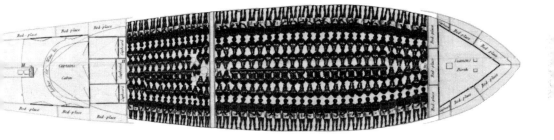

PACKING THE CARGO. You can see from these plans how tightly the ships were packed for the Middle Passage. Some slaves lay in lines, chained head to foot. Others had to crouch on shelves which ran round the hull. Each ledge was only two and a half feet above the other, and one man thought the slaves looked "like books on a shelf." But their places were more like coffins, and indeed many slaves died where they lay. Unwanted babies were sometimes tossed overboard and grief-stricken mothers tried to leap into the water after them.

THE CREW.   Above, you can see a cabin-boy and a ship's carpenter. They suffered on the dreadful voyage almost as much as the slaves. They too died of fever and *flux*. Unlike the slaves, they were not worth any money to the ship's captain if they were alive when they arrived in America. Only tough men or escaping criminals would put up with the months at sea under the captain's whip. Officers feared a mutiny by the crew as much as a slave uprising.

REBELLION. Only a few slaves ever managed to rebel and take over the ship, but captains always feared that it might happen. They tried to mix slaves from one tribe with slaves from different ones. Since they didn't speak the same language, the slaves couldn't plot rebellion. In this picture, the crew are shackling slaves together by the leg. The whip lies ready and the sailors are armed. The slave ships carried cannon to ward off any pirates who might try to capture the ship and its valuable cargo.

KEEPING THEM FIT. Some captains brought their entire shipload of slaves ashore, alive and healthy. One or two boasted that their slaves danced and sang on board. The picture above shows how they usually danced—to a whip. There were nets along the decks to stop the slaves jumping overboard. They were forced to exercise and forced to eat. If a slave tried to starve himself to death, the crew forced his jaws open with a sharp tool and poured the food down his throat.

JOURNEY'S END. The slaves were given just enough food to stay alive during the cruel voyage across the Atlantic. As the ship neared the West Indies, they were fattened up. Their skin was polished with palm oil. Gunpowder was rubbed on their skin to hide any sores or small-pox scars. This was to make them look healthy when they came ashore, like the slaves in the picture opposite.

TO BE SOLD, on board the Ship *Bance-Island*, on tuesday the 6th of *May* next, at *Ashley-Ferry*; a choice cargo of about 250 fine healthy

NEGROES,

just arrived from the Windward & Rice Coast. —The utmost care has already been taken, and shall be continued, to keep them free from the least danger of being infected with the SMALL-POX, no boat having been on board, and all other communication with people from *Charles-Town* prevented.

Austin, Laurens, & Appleby.

N. B. Full one Half of the above Negroes have had the SMALL-POX in their own Country. .

SOLD. Planters crowded to the quayside as soon as they heard that a slave ship had docked. They were attracted by posters like the one opposite which advertised "fine, healthy Negroes." Sometimes a "scramble" was held. The crew darkened the ship by draping the sails around the deck like a tent. The buyers paid a fixed sum of money. Then they rushed on board to grab as many slaves as they could. They even tried to tie their bewildered slaves together with handkerchiefs to stop another buyer snatching them away.

AUCTIONS. The picture below shows slaves landing on shore. They were sold by *auction* to the highest bidder. Buyers looked hard at a slave's teeth to make sure he was young. He might be an old man with his grey hair dyed black. Sick *refuse slaves* were sold first. Doctors sometimes bought weak slaves. They hoped to strengthen them and sell them later at a profit. Hopeless cases were left at the water's edge to die. But the best ones were worth a lot—thousands of pounds in today's money.

THE PROFITS. The Goree warehouses in Liverpool, shown here, were named after an island off the West African coast called Gorée. The warehouses were built right on the quay where slave ships of many nations tied up. The slaver *Enterprize* reached Liverpool in 1804 with a profit of nearly £25,000. The owners of the slave ship *Fortune* were disappointed with the ship's profits in 1805. They had only gained £13,000 from the voyage.

A PROTEST IN LIVERPOOL. Ship owners in Liverpool openly sold slave chains and collars. They said the chains were for "Blacks or Dogs." The town hall was decorated with carvings of Negroes and elephants' teeth. This picture shows fashionable people entering a theatre in Liverpool. A wealthy audience hissed at a drunken actor, George Frederick Cooke, when he shouted from the stage: "I have not come here to be insulted by a set of wretches, every brick in whose infernal town is cemented with an African's blood."

The Plantations

Out of every hundred slaves who were taken captive, about twenty-five died in Africa or on the voyage. The slaves who reached America had just begun their sufferings. In the next two years, a third of the new arrivals died. This was the stage called *seasoning*, when slaves were taught to do their work and to fear the slave driver's whip.

The pictures in this chapter show how slaves lived in the 18th and 19th century. During that time, the living conditions of many slaves improved. And some slaves were luckier than others. In South America, the Catholic Church made sure that slaves had some rights—they could marry in church, and families were kept together. In the West Indies, the Africans were allowed to keep some of their customs, like playing drums. But in the southern states of America, the slaves lost all their rights. Husbands and wives were split up; children were sold away from their mothers. The good slave owners were fond of their slaves, but treated them like children who could not be trusted.

The difference between the poorest whites and the slaves was very small, but it was important. A free man is a person in his own right. No matter how poor, he has some self-respect. A slave, even if he is well-cared for, belongs to someone else. He is property and can be bought and sold like an animal.

MUZZLES AND SHACKLES. When the slaves
first arrived, they were starved, beaten and tortured to
break their spirit. Look at the pictures on the left.
The woman slave in the picture above cannot eat or
drink because she is wearing a muzzle. The man has
his wrist and ankle chained together with an iron
shackle. Below, the slave has a pronged iron collar
fastened around his neck. He cannot turn his head.
If he tries to run away into the woods, the prongs
will catch in the branches.

SLAVE DRIVERS. The planters hired tough white
overseers to get as much work as possible from their
slaves. The overseers had black assistants called slave
drivers, or "dogdrivers." As you can see from the
picture above, the master encouraged the slave
drivers to use their whips freely. Most slave drivers
were cruel men who enjoyed their work. A few just
pretended to whip the slaves. One kindly slave driver
was beaten because he wept at the sight of a slave
his master had murdered.

PUNISHMENT.   Some slaves tried to fight back by starting fires, stealing or pretending to be sick. Sometimes they hurt themselves on purpose or ran away. Sometimes they just got drunk. This picture shows the "House of Correction" in Jamaica. Slaves who disobeyed their masters were cruelly punished. They were lashed with a *cat-o'-nine-tails* and forced to walk a *treadwheel*. Other slaves had to do the whipping.

PLANTATIONS. In the West Indies, the slaves worked on the huge plantations growing sugar cane and making rum. In the southern states of America, they worked mostly in the tobacco and cotton fields. This picture shows slaves picking cotton under a scorching sun. It was hard, back-breaking work. After the cotton was picked, the slaves had to pull the seeds out of the cotton fibres. If a slave worked from dawn to dusk, he could only take the seeds out of one pound of cotton.

THE COTTON GIN. In 1793, an inventor named Eli Whitney happened to stop at a cotton plantation in America. He saw how hard it was for the slaves to pull the seeds out of the cotton fibres. Ten days later, he had invented a machine called the *cotton gin.* You can see a slave using it in this picture. A slave could seed fifty pounds of cotton with it in a day.

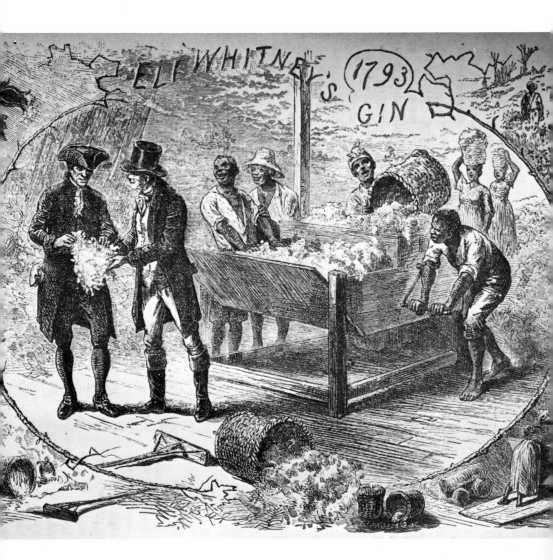

THE DOCKS. After the cotton was seeded, it was packed into bales. The bales were loaded onto steamboats, and shipped down the Mississippi River to the docks. You can see the docks at New Orleans, Louisiana, in this picture. Slaves are unloading the bales of cotton and stacking them on the docks. Then the cotton was packed into bigger ships and sent to cloth factories in the north of America and in England.

FARMERS AND PLANTERS. Many of the white farmers in the southern states of America were almost as poor as the slaves. Other farmers only had two or three slaves. They often worked alongside their *fieldhands* at harvest time. The picture above shows a rich southern gentleman outside his beautiful white mansion. There were not many planters in the South who could afford such a fine home. These few rich planters often had hundreds of slaves working for them.

HOUSE SLAVES. Not all slaves were fieldhands. Others worked at the docks, or in factories in the north of America. There were also house slaves. On small plantations the women, children and old men worked in the house. Rich planters and city folk used slaves as butlers, footmen, cooks, and nannies. Because they lived near the white family, house slaves thought they were better than other slaves. This "dandy" slave dressed in fashionable clothes looks very grand. But if money ran short he would be sold, like the dandy slaves in the picture opposite.

"THE QUARTERS." This photograph shows a slave cabin. On the farms, the slaves lived near the master's house. On the big plantations, the rows of identical slave cabins, called "the quarters," were close to the overseer's cottage. Some good owners gave their slaves well-built and warm cabins. They allowed the slaves to grow vegetables and keep chickens. But most cabins were unheated and leaked when it rained. They had mud floors and the windows had no glass to keep out mosquitos.

TIME OFF. In this picture you can see that the slaves born in captivity enjoyed music and dancing as much as their African ancestors had done. These West Indians have made drums out of barrels. Good planters allowed their slaves to hold a Saturday evening dance, with banjos and fiddles, in their quarters. The slaves also loved African animal stories, and made up their own, like the stories about "Brer Rabbit" outwitting "Brer Fox."

TO BE SOLD & LET

BY PUBLIC AUCTION,

On *MONDAY the* 18th *of* MAY, 1829,

UNDER THE TREES,

FOR SALE,

THE THREE FOLLOWING

SLAVES,

VIZ.

HANNIBAL, about 30 Years old, an excellent House Servant, of Good Character.
WILLIAM, about 35 Years old, a Labourer.
NANCY, an excellent House Servant and Nurse.

The MEN belonging to "LEECH'S" Estate, and the WOMAN to Mrs. D. SMIT

TO BE LET,

On the usual conditions of the Hirer finding them in Food, Clothing and Medical ance,

THE FOLLOWING

MALE and FEMALE

SLAVES,

OF GOOD CHARACTERS,

ROBERT BAGLEY, about 20 Years old, a good House Servant.
WILLIAM BAGLEY, about 18 Years old, a Labourer.
JOHN ARMS, about 18 Years old.
JACK ANTONIA, about 40 Years old, a Labourer.
PHILIP, an Excellent Fisherman.
HARRY, about 27 Years old, a good House Servant.
LUCY, a Young Woman of good Character, used to House Work and the Nursery.
ELIZA, an Excellent Washerwoman.
CLARA, an Excellent Washerwoman.
FANNY, about 14 Years old, House Servant.
SARAH, about 14 Years old, House Servant.

Also for Sale, at Eleven o'Clock,

Fine Rice, Gram, Paddy, Books, Muslins, Needles, Pins, Ribbons, &c. &c.

AT ONE O'CLOCK, THAT CELEBRATED ENGLISH HORSE,

BLUCHER,

SOLD AND LET. If money ran short, masters could always sell or even hire out some of their slaves. They were sold at auctions just as if they were rice or books. The poster on the left is advertising a slave auction in the West Indies. The slaves had no surnames of their own. They took the surname of their owner, and their name changed each time they were bought by a new master. Most slaves were called "boy" or "nigger" or, when they were old, "uncle".

HUSBAND AND WIFE. Sometimes a master forced his slaves to marry. He hoped they would have children so his stock of slaves would grow. In the American South, the marriages were not legal and were usually not held in Church. A slave could marry again if he was sold away from home. One slave preacher made couples vow to love and to cherish "till death or distance us do part." This family on the auction block could be sold to different masters. The father could do nothing to protect his family.

"MAMMIES". This picture shows how planters liked to think about slaves. The black nurse, or "mammy", is playing happily with her master's golden-haired daughter. It was usually not true. The slave nurse was more likely mourning her own babies who had been sold away from her. One rejoiced at her child's death: "Praise God! Praise God! My child is gone to Jesus. That's one child of mine you're never gonna sell." Other nurses poisoned the white children and it is not hard to understand why.

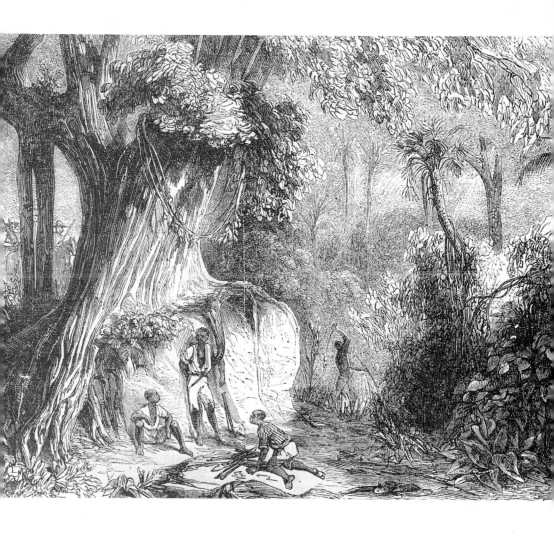

REBELS. Slave owners were always afraid of uprisings. There were usually far more slaves than white men in a district. Here you can see rebel slaves in the West Indies with their only weapons—the machete knives they used for cutting sugar cane. Sometimes white families would be found with their throats cut. A few slaves managed to escape to the hills and woods. They lived there as outlaws and made sudden raids on the plantations. But soldiers usually rounded up the rebels very quickly.

RUNAWAYS.   Look at the pictures on the left. The upper picture shows what happened to runaways. Professional slave hunters, armed with guns and using tracker-dogs, were paid to find them, dead or alive. Southern newspapers ran advertisements for runaways, and they always printed little figures like the ones below. The advertisements are sad to read: "He may have succeeded in getting to his wife." "She is no doubt in the area, where she has many children." "He may be trying to reach his mother." Some *fugitives* managed the long journey to freedom in the North or in Canada.

RELIGION.   Some planters, like the one below, had preachers for their slaves. The planter's family attended the service to make sure the preacher told the slaves to be obedient. Some slaves slipped away from these services and went to prayer meetings of their own. There they sang *spirituals*. The words of the songs came from the Bible but they told about the slaves' misery:

> When Israel was in Egypt's land
>   Let my people go
> Oppressed so hard they could not stand
>   Let my people go

Fighting for Freedom

Shipmasters grew rich from the slave trade. Back in England, merchants and businessmen made a fortune selling sugar, rum, tobacco and cotton. But people began to feel that slavery was wrong. In England, religious groups were the first to protest. The *Quaker* "Society of Friends" condemned slavery in 1724. The Evangelicals were another religious group who thought that all Christians should fight the evils of the slave trade. Many Quakers and Evangelicals formed an *abolition* society to start the fight.

But it was inconvenient to end slavery. The planters in the West Indies and America thought that if they had to pay free men to work for them, it would cost them more to produce rum, tobacco and other goods. They would cost more money in England. The poet William Cowper attacked the people who didn't want to end slavery. He imitated their argument in this poem:

> *I pity them greatly, but I must be mum*
> *For how could we do without sugar and rum?*
> *Especially sugar, so needful we see,*
> *What, give up our desserts, our coffee and tea?*

It took time for ideas to change. Patiently, the *reformers* spoke at meeting after meeting about the cruel and horrible facts of the slave trade. They presented petitions to Parliament condemning slavery. Finally, in 1833, Parliament passed an Act which freed all the slaves in the British Empire.

SLAVES IN ENGLAND.   There were Negro slaves in England, like this man brushing the flies away from his mistress. She might be a slave trader's wife. Slaves in England were sometimes dressed up in fancy silks and turbans. They were even advertised in the newspapers. In 1768, the *Liverpool Chronicle* advertised a "Fine Negro Boy for Sale. Eleven or Twelve Years of Age, talks English very well and can Dress Hair in a tolerable way."

GRANVILLE SHARP. Granville Sharp was a young civil servant who worked in London. This picture shows his meeting, in 1767, with a sick Negro slave called Jonathan Strong. Granville Sharp's brother, James, ran a free surgery in London. Strong visited the surgery and the brothers nursed him back to health. Two years later Strong's master saw him again, fit and healthy. He claimed him back, and sold him to a Jamaican planter. Before he was shipped off, Strong smuggled a message to Granville Sharp who took the case to court. Strong was set free.

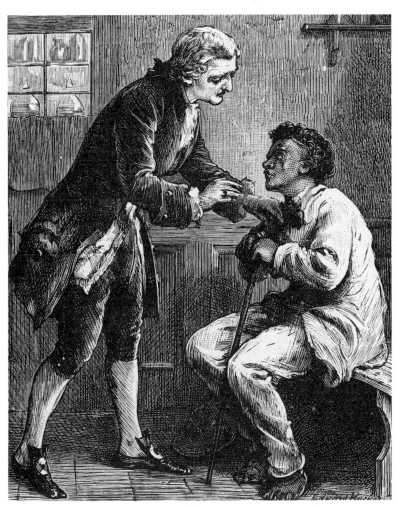

THE MANSFIELD JUDGEMENT. Under English law all men are supposed to be free. Granville Sharp decided to test it. He asked a court of law to say that James Somersett, a runaway slave, was a free man. "Is not a Negro a Man?" he asked. This picture shows Lord Mansfield, who was the Lord Chief Justice of England. He judged the case, and reluctantly decided Sharp was right. "Whatever the inconvenience, . . . as soon as any slave sets foot on English ground, he shall be free." This judgement set free 14,000 Negro slaves who were living in England.

THE ZONG. Captain Collingwood of the Liverpool slave ship *The Zong* threw 132 live slaves overboard in three days. He said it was an act of mercy because disease had broken out on the ship and there was no more water on board. But he really did it because he thought the insurance money would be worth more than the sick slaves. When the insurance company refused to pay, Granville Sharp wanted the captain tried for murder. He failed to bring the case to court, but the captain's action shocked many people's consciences.

JOHN NEWTON.   John Newton, whose picture is shown below, also spoke out against the slave trade. He was the rector of St. Mary Woolnoth, in London, and he wrote several well-known hymns, such as "Amazing Grace." Newton had had an extraordinary life as a white slave and then as a captain of a slave ship. Then he turned against the slave trade, and became a clergyman. His congregation listened wide-eyed to his first-hand accounts of the evil business "at which my heart shudders."

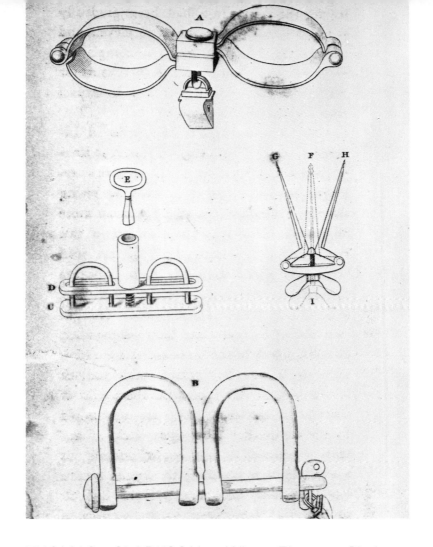

THOMAS CLARKSON. When Thomas Clarkson was still a student, he decided to join the fight to stop the slave trade. He set out to find all the facts about the horrors of the trade. He visited the ports of Liverpool and Bristol, and asked the captains and crews endless questions. In Liverpool he bought slaving manacles and thumbscrews. You can see pictures of these torture instruments above. He published them in an anti-slavery book. Clarkson was almost drowned at Liverpool docks when nine angry seamen tried to push him off the pier head. He was a big, heavy man and he escaped by lowering his great head and charging.

THE ABOLITION SOCIETY. In 1787 Clarkson, Sharp and a group of Quakers and other reformers founded the Society for the Abolition of the Slave Trade. They made an emblem for their society, which you can see here. Josiah Wedgwood, the man who started the famous Wedgwood pottery works, made china medallions showing the emblem. Round the figure of a Negro, kneeling in chains, runs the question: "Am I Not a Man and a Brother?"

ANGRY MERCHANTS. This picture shows the merchants of Liverpool. They did not think of slaves as brothers. They taunted Clarkson by drinking the toast: "Success to the Trade!" The merchants sneered at the Abolition Society. They called the *abolitionists* the "Saints" and claimed they were in the pay of enemy nations. Slavery, they said, could not be ended without financial ruin for English trade. The merchants themselves would lose all their profits. What was more, smokers would get no tobacco and children no sugary sweets!

WILLIAM WILBERFORCE. William Wilberforce, whose picture is shown here, was a charming and popular young M.P. with lots of money. He made some of his profits by employing child-workers in his factories. He liked drinking, gambling and going to parties. But in 1785 he became an Evangelical Christian and took up the cause of abolition. Wilberforce became the leader of the Abolition Society. His position in Parliament and his close friendship with the Prime Minister, William Pitt, helped the movement to become well-known.

ADAM SMITH. Adam Smith was one of the first *economists*. He pointed out that it cost more to feed and house a slave than to hire a free man to do the work. People found other reasons why slaves were no longer needed. Merchants and factory owners were becoming rich from new industries in England like coal, iron and cloth. England now had other supplies of sugar, including her own crop of sugar-beet. As people began to realize that slavery was wrong, they found they could afford to do without it.

THE STRUGGLE FOR ABOLITION. The campaign against the slave trade took twenty years to succeed. Wilberforce, armed with Clarkson's facts, spoke at meeting after meeting. You can see him here making an anti-slavery speech in a crowded hall. M.P.s who did not care about slaves did listen when Wilberforce talked about the wretched lives of British seamen. He proved to them that "more sailors die in one year in the slave trade than die in two years in all our other trades put together."

SUCCESS. Bill after bill was presented to Parliament to end the slave trade. The opposition was fierce. William Pitt and another M.P., Charles James Fox, spoke out in Parliament in favour of the bills. The picture shows Pitt addressing the Commons. At last, in 1807, Parliament passed the bill which abolished dealing and trading in slaves in British territories. The House of Commons rang with cheers. Wilberforce covered his face with his hands while tears poured down his cheeks.

REBELLIONS.   The reformers knew that abolishing the slave trade was not enough. It was still legal for men to own slaves, even if they couldn't buy new ones from Africa. The slaves themselves did not understand the new law. They thought their masters were cheating them because they didn't set them free. Some slaves plotted rebellions. The English settlers in British Guinea hanged 47 rebel slaves. In 1832, 50,000 slaves rose up in Jamaica. They were savagely whipped and the leaders were hanged.

FREEING THE SLAVES. In 1833, Parliament passed another bill which freed all the slaves in the British Empire. "Thank God," said the dying Wilberforce, "that I should have witnessed the day." The planters received £20 million *compensation*. Here you can see the slaves rejoicing as they are told of their freedom. Then the slaves found that they had to work forty hours a week for their old masters for several years without pay. Freedom was not so sweet.

THE "AFRICAN SQUADRON." These pictures show the Royal Navy's "African Squadron" at work. British sailors burned down slave factories on the African coast. After Britain abolished the slave trade in her own territories, the Royal Navy became an international policeman. England signed treaties with other countries which allowed her navy to stop and search foreign ships for illegal slaves. One captain tied his load of slaves to the ship's anchor and dropped them overboard as the British ship approached. Without evidence, no one could take him to court.

ANOTHER VOYAGE. The slaves in the British colonies were now free British citizens. But in the West Indies, the ex-slaves had a hard time finding jobs. The sugar industry was employing fewer workers because it faced competition from South America and the East Indies. These areas were supplying Europe with sugar. Many of the West Indian slaves became the West Indian poor. In recent years, many West Indians have set out on another voyage—this time to England—in the hope of starting a new life.

Free at Last

When the American states broke free from England in 1776, they made a Declaration of Independence. It said that all Americans had the right to "life, liberty and the pursuit of happiness." Thomas Jefferson, who wrote it, was a slave owner himself, but a very good one. He wanted all the slaves to be set free, but the southern slave states would not allow it.

All the same, America banned slave carrying from Africa in 1807, the same year as England. By 1808 the northern states had freed their slaves. Unlike the North, the southern states depended on slaves to work on the cotton plantations and in the tobacco fields. They fought bitterly to keep their four million slaves.

As in England, the Americans were beginning to see that slavery was wrong. Some reformers thought all the Negroes should be sent back to Africa as free men. Some Negroes did return to West Africa, and set up the nation of Liberia. Other reformers wanted the slaves in America to be *emancipated* at once. But they wanted the slaves to continue to work for their old masters for several years. The quarrel between southern slave owners and the northern abolitionists grew very bitter. A bloody civil war broke out before slavery was finally abolished.

But laws cannot change the way people think. The black slaves had been treated with contempt for hundreds of years. They were now free, but still not the equals of the whites. Even today, the problem of *prejudice* against black men has not been completely solved.

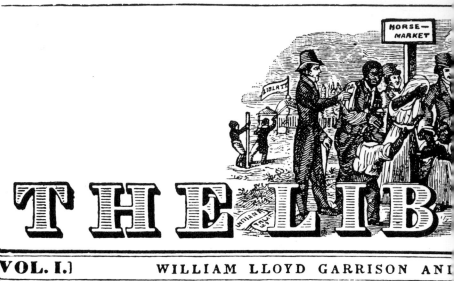

THE LIB

VOL. I.]   WILLIAM LLOYD GARRISON ANI

BOSTON, MASSACHUSETTS.]   OUR COUNTRY IS THE WORLD—OU

THE LIBERATOR. William Lloyd Garrison was an abolitionist who lived in the north of America, in New England. Like many American reformers, he wanted to end slavery right away. In 1831, he began to publish a newspaper in Boston, Massachusetts, called *The Liberator.* He was only twenty-five years old at the time. The picture above shows the title which appeared on the front page of every issue. "I will not retreat a single inch," Garrison said, and "I WILL BE HEARD."

NAT TURNER. Nat Turner was a black preacher who became a great slave hero. He thought he was called by God to lead his people from slavery. In 1831, he and his followers rebelled and murdered sixty white people. The picture opposite shows the slave owners capturing Nat Turner two months later. He was hanged, but the slaves made up a song:

You can't stop the world from turning round
And you can't stop Nat Turner from gaining ground

... R A T O R.

AC KNAPP, PUBLISHERS.   [NO. 22.

TRYMEN ARE MANKIND.   [SATURDAY, MAY 28, 1831.

THE ALTON RIOT. The slave owners hated anyone who was against slavery. An abolitionist named Elijah Lovejoy set up a printing press in Alton, Illinois. He printed anti-slavery books and pamphlets. The picture above shows the slave owners burning the printing press to the ground. They killed Elijah Lovejoy at the same time. Fights broke out between the abolitionists and the slave owners. Both sides became more bitter, and it was hard to find a way to solve the problem of slavery.

THE "UNDERGROUND RAILROAD." The picture on the right shows Quakers helping runaway slaves to escape to the North or Canada. The Quakers helped to set up an "Underground Railroad." It wasn't a railway at all—just a chain of homes where runaways could stop on their journey to freedom. One escaped slave named Harriet Tubman risked her life to help three hundred other slaves to freedom on the "Underground Railroad." She dressed up the slaves as ladies, in Big Quaker sunbonnets and veils. She went with them, pretending to be their slave.

THE NORTH STAR Frederick Douglass was a slave who managed to escape to freedom. He ran an anti-slavery newspaper called *The North Star*. It was called that because slaves who were running away were told to follow the north star to Canada. Douglass was scornful of the American Declaration of Independence which said that all men were created equal. How could this be, he asked, when Americans were allowed to hunt, shoot and kill runaway slaves in their own country?

ESCAPES.　The northern states abolished slavery in 1808. One light-skinned Negress named Ellen Croft dressed herself up as a white man. Then she took her darker-skinned husband into freedom in the North, by saying he was her slave. If you look carefully at the picture below, you can see for yourself how a slave named Henry Box Brown got away. Then the American government passed a new law. Any slave who escaped to the North had to be returned to his owner in the South.

THE RESURRECTION OF HENRY BOX BROWN AT PHILADELPHIA.
Who escaped from Richmond Va in a Box 3 feet long 2½ ft deep and 2 ft wide

UNCLE TOM'S CABIN. In 1852, Harriet Beecher Stowe published a book about the horrors of slave life called *Uncle Tom's Cabin*. It was a best-seller in America and England. The next year, Mrs. Stowe travelled to England to talk at anti-slavery meetings. The picture on the left shows the real Uncle Tom, an escaped slave called Josiah Henson. Harriet Beecher Stowe had read his life-story and based her own novel on his life.

UNCLE TOM. Some black people in America today call a black man an "Uncle Tom" if he tries too hard to please white people. The picture above from *Uncle Tom's Cabin* shows why. Uncle Tom does not fight back when his owner decides to sell him. He just accepts his fate and prays to God to forgive his cruel master. Somehow, the long years of slavery made many slaves think their way of life was normal. Some of them even thought they were robbing their masters if they ran away.

HARPER'S FERRY. John Brown was a strange man who took up the fight against slavery when he was fifty-five years old. In 1858, he planned an armed uprising to set up a new government. He would be the head of the government and would free all the slaves. He decided to raid a government arms store at Harper's Ferry, Virginia, to get guns and ammunition for the uprising. But the raid was a complete failure. Brown and his followers were arrested and sentenced to death.

JOHN BROWN'S BODY. In his prison cell, John Brown wrote letters and articles against slavery. Many people thought he was a mad troublemaker, but others felt great loyalty to him because of his battle to end slavery. On his way to the gallows he stopped to kiss a Negro baby, as the picture opposite shows. Several years later, northern soldiers marched off to fight in the Civil War singing:

John Brown's body lies a-moulderin' in the grave
But his soul goes marching on

82

THE CIVIL WAR. This map shows the American states in 1856. The slave states are marked in black and the free states in white. The land in the West that was still unsettled is shown in grey. The southerners wanted slaves to be allowed in the Western territories. The northerners wanted the West to become free states, like California. In 1861 the southern states declared their independence and formed the Confederate States of America. The quarrel between North and South had grown into civil war.

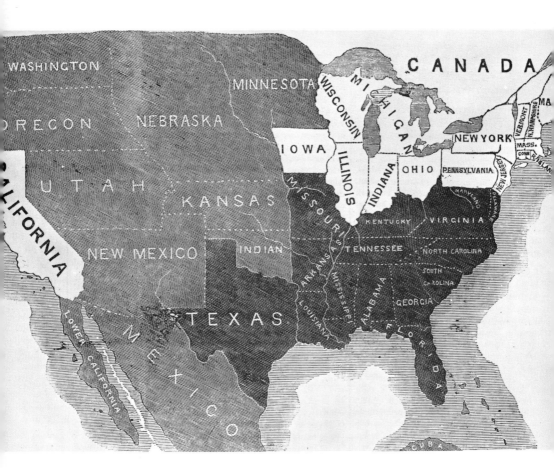

BLACK SOLDIERS. Free Negroes who lived in the North joined the northern, or Union, army. You can see them enlisting in the picture. Southern slaves also joined the Union army because they could gain their freedom that way. They crept up to the army camp at night, calling to the soldiers not to shoot. "Open your gates and let some contraband in!" they shouted. They became known as *contrabands*, because they were smuggled in illegally. In the South, planters used their loyal slaves to build forts against the Union troops.

ABRAHAM LINCOLN. The photograph opposite shows President Abraham Lincoln (1809–65) and his small son Tad. Lincoln did not think southerners had the right to leave the United States and set up their own government. He wanted above all to save the union of all the American states. He knew that slavery had to be abolished. "As a nation we began by declaring: 'all men are created equal,'" he wrote. "But now we say, 'all men are created equal except Negroes'."

FREE AT LAST. Lincoln declared that from 1st January, 1863 all slaves in the South were "henceforward and forever free." The picture above shows him signing the declaration, which was called the "Emancipation Proclamation." In 1865, the Confederate States surrendered. Lincoln tried to make his peace terms generous. He knew it would be hard for southern planters to get used to their new lives without slaves. Several weeks after the Civil War ended, Lincoln was *assassinated* by a half-mad actor who favoured the Confederate States.

HOW FREE? The newly-freed slaves held joyful celebrations. Then they tried to find work. The plantations were ruined and the white mansions burned to the ground. One black said later on: "Tents all gone, no place to stay and nothing to eat. That was the big freedom." The southerners blamed the Negroes for their defeat. They joined secret societies like the Ku Klux Klan which terrorized and *lynched* any Negroes who tried to vote or to own property. A new struggle began—for *civil rights.*

WHITES ONLY. Some whites thought that black people were not their equal. In place of slavery came *segregation.* The conductor in the picture opposite is telling a black man to leave the railway carriage because it is reserved for whites. The Negro was no longer a slave but he was not a first-class citizen. In some states, he had to send his children to separate schools and travel in special carriages on the trains. White men tried to stop him from voting.

CIVIL RIGHTS. In America, the blacks carried on their struggle for civil rights for one hundred years. In the early 1960s, blacks in the South held "sit-ins" at lunch counters. They organized marches and demonstrations, which sometimes turned violent. This photograph shows a policeman with a dog watching a demonstration for civil rights in an American city. Finally, in 1965, the American government passed a law which stated that all blacks in America had the right to eat in any restaurant and to sit anywhere they wanted in a train or bus. But even today, blacks in America and in England are still fighting for equal treatment.

Table of Dates

New Words

Abolition	Doing away with a custom or practice, like slavery
Abolitionist	Someone who wants to abolish a custom or practice
Agent	Representative of a person or business firm; person who does the actual work
Assassinate	To kill someone by violence and treachery
Auction	Public sale where goods are sold to the highest bidder
Cat-o'-nine tails	A whip with nine knotted lashes
Civil rights	The rights of every citizen guaranteed by law
Compensation	Money paid to a person for giving something up
Contraband	Goods smuggled into a country during wartime; Negro slaves who worked in the northern army camps during the Civil War
Cotton gin	Machine which pulled the seeds out of the cotton fibres
Economist	Someone who studies how goods are produced and how money is used
Emancipate	To set free
Fieldhand	Farm worker
Flux	Name for dysentery, a severe form of diarrhoea

Fugitive	A runaway
Indentured labourer	Someone who agreed to work without pay for seven years in return for his fare to America
Lynch	To hang someone without a legal trial
Molasses	Treacly syrup left over when sugar crystals are made; used for making rum
Overseer	Someone who directs workmen. On the plantations, the man who made sure the slaves did their work
Pagan	Someone who does not believe in the Christian God.
Plantation	Estate in America where sugar, cotton or tobacco was grown
Prejudiced	To hold an opinion against someone without good reason
Reformer	Someone who wants to improve or change a bad state of affairs
Refuse slaves	Slaves who were sick or crippled after the Middle Passage
Quaker	Member of a religious group known for their peacefulness and plain way of dressing
Seasoning	To make something or someone fit, to prepare. In America, the training period when slaves were taught their jobs
Segregation	Separating one group of people from the rest of the community
Spirituals	Religious songs sung by American Negroes
Treadwheel	A revolving wheel with steps on it. As a punishment, slaves were forced to tread the steps, walking round and round

More Books

Fekere, Irene. *Lincoln Frees the Slaves* (Macdonald, 1971). The story behind President Lincoln's "Emancipation Proclamation," which finally ended slavery in America.

Fritz, Jean. *Brady* (Gollancz, 1966). An exciting story about a boy named Brady who finds out that his father is helping slaves to escape to freedom on the Underground Railroad.

Lester, Julius. *To Be a Slave* (Longman Young Books, 1970). This book includes the life-stories of ex-slaves and interviews with them. In their own words, Negroes tell what it was like to be a slave.

Lomax, Alan. *The Penguin Book of American Folk Songs* (Penguin, 1968). Here are many of the spirituals which the slaves sang on the plantations in the American South.

Martin, Bernard. *John Newton and the Slave Trade* (Longman Then and There Series, 1961). The story of John Newton and his fight to end the slave trade.

Stowe, Harriet Beecher. *Uncle Tom's Cabin* (Blackie, 1970). A famous story about slave life which turned many people against slavery one hundred years ago.

Twain, Mark. *Huckleberry Finn* (Blackie, 1965). When Huckleberry Finn runs away from home, he takes his slave, Jim, with him. He learns not to feel guilty about taking Jim away.

Index

Picture Credits

The Publishers wish to thank the following for their kind permission to reproduce copyright illustrations on the pages mentioned: Mansell Collection, jacket, 6, 13, 14—15, 17, 19, 32, 33, 40, 46, 47, 50, 68, 75, 82, 83, 84; Mary Evans Picture Library, 8, 9, 10, 12, 15, 16, 20, 21, 22, 25, 29, 30, 31, 34, 35, 38 (top), 39, 43, 44 (top), 51, 52 (bottom), 53, 54, 56, 57, 63, 64, 65, 67, 69, 72, 74—75, 76, 77, 80, 85, 89; Radio-Times Hulton Picture Library, 11, 18, 24, 36, 38 (bottom), 42, 48, 49, 52 (top), 58, 59, 60, 66, 71, 78, 81, 87, 88; National Maritime Museum, London, 27, 28; Josiah Wedgwood & Sons, Ltd. 62; Library of Congress, Washington, 79; U.S.I.S., 86; Associated Press, 90. Other pictures appearing in this book are the property of the Wayland Picture Library.